Mayflower
BEYOND THE HORIZON
1620–2020

Anthology of Young People's Writing 2019

 **UPP**

University of Plymouth Press

The Mayflower Steps on the Barbican in Plymouth UK, built in 1934, are close to the sight where the *Mayflower* is believed to have set sail in 1620.

Paperback edition first published in the United Kingdom in 2019 by University of Plymouth Press, Roland Levinsky Building, Drake Circus, Plymouth, Devon, PL4 8AA, United Kingdom.

ISBN 9781841024356

A CIP catalogue record of this book is available from the British Library.

Managing Editor: Amy Potter
Editor: Laura Roberts
Publishing Assistants: Stephany Choremi, Lucinda Hensley, Kate Marler, Charlotte Pett, Rui Shen
Publisher: Paul Honeywill UPP
Photographer: Alan Stewart
Cover artwork: Maisy Edmonds

Printed and bound by Short Run Press, Exeter, UK.

With contributions from University of Plymouth English with Publishing BA (Hons) Students, who ran workshops in the schools: Connor Hansford, Danielle Tremeer, Eilish Macbeth, Ffion Edwards, Georgia O'Neil, Isla Nunne, Jessica Ford, Jessica Curtis-Jouxson, Kathryn Gandy, Kathryn Whatley, Rebecca Harker, Shanelle Spanton, Sophie Muir-Harris

This anthology is sponsored by the University of Plymouth and supported by Plymouth City Council.

Foreword

As a woman serving in today's Royal Navy and as a history graduate, it is a pleasure to commend this book depicting our rich female maritime history. This remarkable anthology is the work of children from two Plymouths – our Devonian Ocean City here in the UK and the city which inhabits the site of the first Pilgrim settlement in Massachusetts, USA. The strong and mutually beneficial ties that Plymouth (UK) maintains with our American cousins is nicely reflected in this project, as they are in the work to bring the *Mayflower* 400 celebrations together on both sides of the Atlantic Ocean in 2020.

I have been particularly struck by how this centenary has provided the chance to look at this important chapter in Plymouth's past from different perspectives – in this case from the experience of the women involved, brought to life through the writings and drawings of the next generation.

My own seafaring career began in 1993 at the gates of Britannia Royal Naval College. I followed in the footsteps of members of the Women's Royal Naval Service, the WRNS, who recently celebrated their own Centenary having been established in 1918. Today's fully integrated Royal Navy is a diverse and inclusive Service, where every form of employment is open to anyone regardless of their gender, social background, ethnicity, religious views or sexual orientation. Over my career women have proved themselves, as Regulars and Reserves, at sea in the surface fleet and onboard our Royal Fleet Auxiliary ships, in the air in the Fleet Air Arm and under the sea in the Submarine Service. They are now training to become Royal Marine Commandos. I am proud to stand among so many pioneering women and the highly professional men with which we serve to protect our nation's interests.

I hope this book will contribute further to our understanding of the contribution women have made and continue to make to our maritime heritage.

Commodore Ellie Ablett MBE MA Royal Navy.

Commodore Ablett read Modern History at Somerville College, Oxford and joined the Royal Navy in 1993 among the first wave of women joining the Service after its amalgamation with the Women's Royal Naval Service and is one of the most senior women in the Navy.

Beyond the Horizon

Fear washed over me,
Tidal wave of emotion.
Today is my day,
My future,
My beginning,
Unravelling like a ribbon
Thrown into the wind.

Blankets of grass,
Cover sleeping islands.
Blankets of clouds,
Blinding light peering through,
Bouncing off glassy seas.
Unexplored dimensions,
Full of mysterious creatures,
Neon fish,
And my dreams.

Faint calls for help,
Winds talking to me,
Then deafening silence.
It is cut by the
Screech of birds above and around.

Kayla Thindwa
Age 10

The *Sea Dragon*

In August 2017, a small group of women from the University of Plymouth sailed around the UK on a boat called the *Sea Dragon* as they wanted to raise awareness of plastic pollution. During their 30-day mission, they wanted to clear the plastic from the sea.

On the first day, they saw the beautiful sea and the dolphins were jumping up and down. Gentle, warm wind was pushing their sail and made the *Sea Dragon* travel faster. The buildings were getting smaller and soon the Plymouth Hoe was left behind. The waves were gently hitting the sides of the boat and it was peaceful.

In the evening, the black clouds covered the sky and the storm began. The boat was rocking like a person on a seesaw. The boat almost tipped over. They put on their life jackets and quickly ate their tea. Everyone on the boat felt seasick as the waves arched above the *Sea Dragon*. Soon it began to rain, and the crew put their hoods up. There was a stormy night ahead.

Corey Tucker
Age 7

Beyond the Horizon

There was no going back,
When the ship started to sail,
The nerves were shaking in my bones,
The horizon gripping me more and more.

Another dimension full of joy,
Undiscovered, untouched animals,
Roaming the sleepy sandy, islands
With tall stalking pine trees.

My heart full of joy,
My eyes as bright as sapphire.
I couldn't believe it,
I was past the horizon and the phoenixes are chirping
in the dark, desolate island lost on the jungle.

Tyler Parker

Royal Air Force, Commonwealth & Allied Air Forces 1939 – 1945 Memorial. These men and women saved the UK from invasion in 1940.

The Mayflower

The *Speedwell* was moored to the land by a long piece of rope. It was not going anywhere. Vincent stood with his arms folded across his chest. He looked calm and relaxed (but inside his rage burned hotter than the devil's flame). Cathy, Vincent's mother, was boarding the ship when she spotted him. Smiling weakly, she limped over to him.

"Vincent, why aren't you boarding the ship like everyone else?" she questioned. Vincent furrowed his eyebrows and thought about the bigger picture.

"Oh, I don't know – maybe one hundred and one Christians are boarding a cargo ship for six months that isn't made for people!" He replied sarcastically.

After much convincing, Vincent finally agreed to board the ship. However, this did not stop him from dragging his heels to slow them both down. Cathy and Vincent joined the queue but before he could board, she bent down to come within inches of his ear.

"I know it's..." Cathy began but Vincent stomped onto the *Mayflower* before she could finish. Steven, Vincent's dad, was awaiting them within the pungent fumes of the decks. As soon as he saw his family, he detected something was wrong.

"What is wrong with him?" whispered Steven to Cathy.

"He does not want to go to the New World" she mumbled back a bit too loudly.

"Yes, you are right, I don't want to go to the New World with some weird strangers, I hate you, I hate you all!" Screamed Vincent. He stomped his foot down in anger. The ship was silent.

"Would anyone like to play dice?" asked Steven. Despite this being a question, nobody answered.

Konnor Grills
Age 10

Beyond the Stars

The window was dusty, so I got up, raised my arm and wiped it down. At
that moment in time I lived in a flat – a nice one. Not one of those ones
that were in fact very grotty and stinky. I raised my eyes and looked up.
Well, what a sight it was. Stars were shining, the moon was up, and the
sun was down. It was one of those feelings that made me want to run out
there and just catch them all in my pocket. I would catch every single one
apart from the North Star, the most special one of all. The most sparkling
and dazzling one of all. But just remember, it doesn't matter who you are
or where you are because you can do anything and achieve anything!

Claudia Jenkins
Age 9

Beyond the Horizon

Beyond the horizon,
I leave an image of Plymouth.
Leaving the sound of waves gently rolling inwards,
The feeling of shimmering sand between my toes.
Whilst poppies dance in the welcoming breeze.
Towering tall and guiding ships away,
Stands the heart of it all; stands Smeaton's Tower.
Overlooking the clear, coral, blue sea,
The flags roar in the whistling wind,
Standing proud like a group of soldiers,
Clutching the sound of the birds in the morning.
Remembering the place, I call home.

Roxanna Davies
Age 10

The Elizabethan Gardens were built in the 16th century when wealthy merchants were building their houses on the Barbican.

Beyond the Horizon

Time has stopped,
Sailing across a sky-blue sky
Of eternity
Has taken its toll.
Our boat being brutally tossed
By the power of a hundred waves.

Blazing sun falls,
Just like our spirit and hope.
But when we get there,
We'll start a new life.

Preserved food,
Bitter by taste and smell.
Trepidation of death on mind,
The pressure is crushing.

As each day goes on,
I hear voices.
Our New World,
I'll call it America.

Teighlund Reynolds
Age 11

This extension to the
Navy memorial was
designed by Sir Edward
Maufe and sculpted by
Charles Wheeler and
William McMillan in
1954.

Awake

Darkness
Silence
I lie awake
Staring
Out of the window
At the black sky
Of nothingness
I close my tired eyes
Waiting
For sleep to come
But my brain stays alert
I long for summer mornings
To feel the sun's breath
On my neck
And feel the fingers of warmth
Wrap
Around me
The wind roars
the house rattles
I pull the blankets closer
The only thing awake
Was me
And the snow
Falling
Down
Down
Down

Emily Lunney
Age 13

Within the Words

Illustrations dye the page
Like a field of flowers
A work of art.

Every phrase
An assortment of delight
Like a box of chocolates.

Every book is a new adventure
You chase the character's stories
Their lives
And their setbacks.

When you finish
a feeling of accomplishment
But also longing
For the adventures yet to happen
The words
Yet to be written.

Emma Richer
Age 13

Artwork by Holly Melmoth
Age 8

City of Discovery

In the city of discovery, I found
A lighthouse shining bright in the pitch-black night
Standing tall and proud, watching the ships go by.
A dependable eye for the sailor's survival.

In the city of discovery, I saw
The shimmery waves of the calm green sea
The winter waves smashing against the solid rocks,
And the summer seas calmly stroking the gritty sand.

In the city of discovery, I found
The greatest football team scoring magnificent goals against their opponents.
Taking risks to win for their city, to bring home the trophy.

Mason Jones
Age 10

Beyond the Horizon

Excited and gold as I am leaving Plymouth.
Hungry and green in the cramped deck.
Scared and grey as the storm hits.
Happy and yellow as I see the horizon.
Beyond the horizon, there are coloured flowers.
Relaxed and blue when I get off the boat.
Beyond the horizon, life will be good.
Calm and silver as I sleep in the moonlight.

Harry Adkins
Age 6

Sky

The sun wakes up
And gets out of bed;
It goes to the sky
Where his night will end.

He gets kind of sleepy
And heads back down
Soon...

The moon wakes up
And climbs in the sky;
He's wide awake
and looking down.

He gets sleepy
And heads off to bed.

The stars come up
And dance.

Bella Bletzer
Age 10

Built on the
Eddystone Reef in
1759, sections of the
Lighthouse were moved,
stone by stone, in the
1800s to its prominent
position on the Hoe.

The Bird in the Cage

The lie, the mystery, the mask of happiness
Like a bird in a cage
Trapped
Scarred
Weak
Broken
Surrounded
Crowded
People come near and far
To take a piece
A feather
Destroying it
Plucking it and plucking it
But not everyone gets a feather
Since the greedy
Self-absorbed
Jealous
Take it and don't give it to the ones who need it
Once everyone leaves
Whether they ensnared it
Or not
The bird is left
Broken
Bruised
Bare
Happiness: the deceitful lie

Paige Morlan
Age 13

Beyond the Horizon

The tall, towering lighthouse, stood proudly,
Looking like a giant barber pole, watching over the
peaceful sea pounding against the small ancient steps
that would have been used nearly 400 years ago.

The proud, fluttering flags watch over as children,
big and small, play happily every day on the soft
emerald green grass that trails down into the aqua
blue Plymouth Lido.

Louis Rodwell-Chai
Age 10

Beyond the Horizon

The trepidation,
The perpetual peril,
Like time has stopped,
Like a deer in the headlights,
Like millions of years passing.

The crashing waves,
The squawking gulls,
A bustle of crew,
The whistling winds,
Talking to me,
A rustle of the bird's nest.

The rainbow of colours,
Dawn growing,
The sun smirking,
The never-ending
Journey to the horizon.

The aftertaste
Of rotten meals,
The salty air,

Vomit, excrement, urine,
The foul odour
Of dirty people.

Oh, I wonder,
What is there
Of the dreams
Everyone has,
The succulent spices,
The freshly hunted meat.

That is what's beyond
The horizon.

Maisy Edmonds
Age 10

The *HMS Windsor Castle* figurehead of Queen Victoria, made in 1854, has resided at the Plymouth Naval Base Museum since 2001.

A Scene from the City I Love

I look out over the Hoe and what do I see?
Happy children fearlessly trying to climb a tree,
Giggling figures in the distance, splashing in the sea,
The majestic statue of Sir Francis Drake staring up to the sky,
Nearby monuments standing to attention.
Hot and hungry families at ice cream vans in little crowds,
Tourists bathing in the sun, staring at the puffy clouds,
On grass as fresh as broccoli,
Stretching across the seafront like a luxurious carpet
Dotted with day-trippers enjoying picnics and games.
A café full of the scent of scrummy snacks, swarming with people
By the colossal lighthouse in its red and white uniform,
Staring out at Drake's Island,
Across the glittering turquoise sea.
With boats bobbing happily on the surface,
Some sailing towards the horizon with determination,
Leaving behind a scene of beauty.
The coast of the city I love.

Soloman Dean
Age 8

Francis Drake sailed
from Plymouth in 1577
and landed in America
in 1579. He returned
to Plymouth in 1580
having circumnavigated
the globe.

The City of Discovery

In the city of discovery, I smelt,
Plymouth's perfect coffee,
Plymouth's premium pasties,
And bubbling baked beans.

In the city of discovery, I saw,
Chips constantly cracking,
People peacefully chatting,
And fireworks flickering.

In the city of discovery, I heard,
The sea silently crashing,
Builders brilliantly building,
And navy ships slowly sailing.

In the city of discovery, I tasted,
Marshmallows melting gradually,
Fresh fried fish and chips,
And incredible indulgent ice cream.

Joshua Ferreira
Age 10

Stormy Waters

Violent waves,
Ready to attack,
Like a fearless tiger,
Pouncing on its prey,
Slicing, destroying, tearing!

Vicious hurricanes,
Tossing innocent boats around,
Like garbage onto a tip,
Showing no mercy,
Grabbing, threatening, roaring!

Deadly kraken,
Strangling its victim,
Like a medieval hangman's noose,
Suffocating slowly,
Destroying, killing, screaming!

Paulie Saunders
Age 10

Artwork by Liam Dann
Age 11

Mayflower 400

There's No Going Back

Everyday sunset glows, everyday darkness follows. Everyday the sun gets hotter and everyday new life begins. Oceana and Aisa didn't care about the sun or the moon, life or death. All they cared about was the water. It was like their home and the fish were like their family. They explored new species and caves hidden in the distance. At a young age, the twins would go swimming in the pool with their parents, but by the age of four they were swimming in the ocean outside their house. At the age of eight, they were allowed to swim by themselves (no adult supervision). The twins are now ten and today something was coming their way.

Jessica Horton
Age 10

The Deadly Chase

The mermaid, Natasha, was starting to lose hope, was she ever going to catch this ship? She had been chasing it for hours and didn't think she'd ever catch it. She had to tell the Captain about why he should turn immediately! Or else they would go too far. Then it would be too late to save them, they'd be gone...eaten!

This was good, the ship was slowing down. The good news was she was going to catch it, but the bad news was, had they gone too far?

Finally, she had made it! Natasha climbed onto the ship, her tail now transformed to legs as she was on land. She couldn't see anyone. She looked everywhere...
NOTHING!

Jamie Best
Age 10

The Kraken

She turned her gaze upon the sea. It was a soggy day, but she could sense there was something wrong. She didn't know. She pulled out her telescope, but she had no luck. It was getting late, so she went to bed, she hoped with all her heart that it was nothing bad.

Suddenly, the boat crashed against the waves. She woke up, heart pounding. She went outside to see what was going on but to her surprise it all stopped. Confused, worried, terrified, she sat down thinking about what went on that morning but the only things she thought of were things that didn't even exist: sea monsters. The weather was clearer, and she saw long, red arm-like tentacles coming out of the water. Her heart skipped a beat...

She ran back to her room thinking and searching for something that could stop it. She could hit it with her sword, but that wouldn't be very effective. All of a sudden, she had an idea, she had a trumpet which she had used in the past to scare away sharks! But would it work on octopuses? She ran outside with the trumpet and blew as hard as she could. To her surprise, it worked! As quick as a flash the octopus fell under the water, never to be seen again.

Joseph Austen
Age 9

Mayflower

Dear Diary,

On board the *Mayflower*, I'm feeling dreadfully sick. It's the incredibly loud noise of the children playing Cat's Cradle and screaming after they have won, it's giving me a headache. I've been on the *Mayflower* for at least 15 days, but I have around 25 left! I'm sitting in my very uncomfortable bed, dreaming of a better life in the New World. It's so cramped in the orlop deck it's making me feel claustrophobic, you can't blame me – everyone sleeps on this deck. During the calm, gentle seas we all ate beef and vegetable stew. It was so delicious and warm. It made me feel safe and less panicked. I didn't want to go on the top deck today. I couldn't even if I wanted to. As the savage storms began, we couldn't eat the stew. Instead, we had to eat hard biscuits or dried fruit. We all huddled up as the Captain said, "There's 102 passengers on this boat" and everyone was surprised.

Emillie Butler
Age 9

Beyond the Horizon

I am waiting for the *Mayflower* ship
I can smell the wood
I feel worried because I might be sick
I can see the waves splashing against the walls
and I can see the seagulls pecking at the food.

Isabella Mayer
Age 5

Go, go, go!

Over here, come along with me,
Let's take a dip into the salt blue sea,
Dress into your gear, let's go and explore,
What might be waiting for us on the ocean floor?

Hey, look at this,
I think that we found a starfish,
Look at its endless spots, oh nice,
Like a photo worth an unlimited price!

Come on, let's explore more,
Whoa, look at that creature soar,
Yes, it's a majestic manta ray,
Pushing forwards with no time to stop and play!

Hey, stop don't move so fast,
A giant whale is coming past,
Just look at how fast it swims,
Effortless, all because of his gigantic fins!

Yes you, jump on in,
Dive into the deep and swim, swim, swim!
A new world awaits down below,
Magic and wonder... so, go, go go!

Jessica Grant
Age 9

The Mayflower

Scared yet brave, we decided to go.
To discover new things,
A new world
A new home.

Brave but scared, we're ready to go,
Climbing up the mast with a 'heave-ho'.
As the team we pulled the sail,
Together as strong as a whale.

Lily Coote
Age 8

In a Small Boat

Above the sea, thunder claps
Try to deafen my ears
And the clouds try to blind my eyes
With their rainy tears.

And on this night, I try to row
My small wooden boat on the cruel waves
While the water drips from my body
Till I get sight of a spotlight and men.
Somebody waves!

Lewis Elliot
Age 10

Beautiful Plymouth

I look out to Plymouth and what do I see?
Rows of trees with their leaves dancing in the wind.
The sparkling sea, glowing in the burning sun.
The grass sprinkled with lime glitter,
The rose and daisies as beautiful as butterflies.
Jubilant children splashing in the sparkling sea.
Smiling people watching the magnificent sea,
Joyful kids eating lovely ice cream.
A row of flags waving,
Fluffy clouds like cotton candy floating in the sky.
Mums pushing babies in strollers
Along the seafront of beautiful Plymouth.

Sofia Fabian
Age 8

Battle Under the Sea

Sail into the unknown seas,
Rumble, crash and roar,
Crumbling hopes and dreams into sand.

Live your dreams,
For, on one clear day,
You may stand on the endless horizon.

Rumble, rumble, rumble!

The wind sings a deadly song,
Live life on the ocean edge,
Wide enough for all that you can imagine.

Crash, crash, crash!

Crashing waves, violently drown,
While ruthless rain thrashes down,
Destroying the helpless, lonely boats,
As adventures crumble and no longer float.

Roar, roar, roar!

Boz Sivrev
Age 9

In the City of Discovery

In the city of discovery, I see,
Drake's bowls battering each other
The view of the aggressive Armada
And the sinister screams of the Spanish saying El Draco!

In the city of discovery, I see,
The port vomiting into the sea,
Bombs beginning to drop, damaging the land
And the bombed-out church standing tall, watching woefully the changes around it.

In the city of discovery, I see,
Excellent explorers cautious of a perfect patterned lighthouse,
It's light like a gleam of gold.
And Scott from the Antarctic waving goodbye.

In the city of discovery, I see and feel,
The round, rare cobbles in the Barbican, smooth like a baby's cheek
The green seaweed leaving the shore
And the cold ice cream freezing my teeth.

Julia Warjas
Age 10

Artwork by Rhys Walsh
Age 9

Beyond the Horizon

The foamy, icy blue waves lap the sides of the rocks, desperately trying to reach the lush land. The huge version of Santa's hat looks out across the sparkling ocean and a fresh salty scent fills the cool, refreshing air. Sir Francis Drake guards the war memorial as it towers above the small children circling it, wishing to play with them.

Drake's Island hovers above the enormous piece of blue stained glass, its apple green shield protecting it from the water.

I look back at Plymouth as it fades away into the distance. My journey has begun.

Bella Martyn
Age 10

The Sixty-Sixth Day

Hope is almost lost forever,
Being without my family.
No fresh air to let me breathe,
I shout help one more time.
Then a voice calls me,
Saying, "land ahoy!"
Relief filled my empty soul,
A new life awaits me,
And nothing can stop me now.

Samantha Kellett
Age 9

A Wonderful Adventure of the Pilgrim Fathers

6th September 1620

Dear Diary,

As the sun rose, I could feel the anxiety washing over me, like huge crashing waves. I frantically grabbed my bags and waited to be escorted to the harbour.

The mucky streets were full of market people selling their valuables to each other, watching the marvellous *Mayflower* getting ready to sail in the peaceful sea. I grabbed my bag and lugged it to the hard, stone steps. As I was escorted to where I was sleeping, I looked at the amazing view of the calm blue sea. The bright, scorching, orange sun was shining down on me. I went to see if I was allowed some food on the upper deck.

Eloise Farley
Age 10

Poems hide

Poems hide on
My grandparents' porch
And the hoot of an owl
Waiting to be heard
They are in the breeze
That whistles through the trees.

Poems hide in the
Water that flows through the small creek
But when they are noticed
The hoot turns into a howl
And the breeze into a wind
And the water that flows through the small creak
Turns into a raging flood.

Conner Dias
Age 13

Being Happy

Silence falls.
A single dragonfly dips down,
Making a singular ripple.
The breaking sunrise,
Shimmers upon my face.
Sitting by the pond,
In your warm embrace
Being happy.

Ruby Blackwell
Age 13

'The Tribute of Plymouth To Her Glorious Dead' World War I and World War II Memorial.

In the City of Discovery

In the city of discovery, I heard,
The faint footstep of a familiar figure walking down the
Mayflower Steps,
The Armada flags leaving home
And the whispers of a famous statue.

In the city of discovery, I felt,
The bumpiness of cobbles like popcorn popping under my feet,
The smoothness of an explorer's bag
And the echo of the name El Draco called by the spirits
of the Spanish.

In the city of discovery, I saw,
The flickering fireworks fly off and explode,
The church set on fire
And the muffled voices of the wind.

In the city of discovery, I felt,
The sadness of Scott of the Antarctic
Slowly and silently suffering death,
The excitement of the Pilgrim Fathers
Setting off to the New World
And the happiness of the sun
Appearing from the clouds.

Veronica Kubica
Age 10

The Mayflower

As I take a big step onboard the *Mayflower*,
A cold feeling shudders through my body.

I am scared but excited,
I can't wait to see the wonderful world that is
Outside Plymouth.

Everyone is so happy to be able to start a new life,
And all the children are just happy to be playing.

Finally, we set off,
We see all our friends and family waving goodbye,
And as they are out of sight,
The Captain says, "down to the harbour deck now,
hurry!"

Sadly, there isn't much room down here,
Everyone is squished in together.

Everyday the *Mayflower* is a storm,
Day after day,
Night after night.

Yesterday, a little baby was born,
Luckily, there was a doctor on board,
Or else who knows what could have happened?

Every night it gets colder and colder,
And sickness is spreading around.

The food they give us is like prison food,
Sloppy and disgusting.

We eventually stop,
But we can't leave the ship because it's winter.

There is snow everywhere,
So, we will stay onboard.

Some time has passed now,
Along with some people too.

The stench of the ship is appalling,
When the spring comes, we plan to go and build
houses,
But for now, we will stay here.

Finally, the time has come,
Spring is here.

As we wander off the ship,
We decide to find food.

Unfortunately, we don't know how to hunt,
As we wander through the long grass,
There are people.

Happily, we run like cheetahs towards them,
Their names are Tisquantum and Squants.

Over the next month they help us
Hunt, build and survive.

Eventually, the *Mayflower* sailed back to Plymouth,
England.

Evie Richards

Beyond the Horizon

Beyond the horizon,
I leave behind an image of Plymouth
The scattered grey hard rocks safely protecting our home.
I leave behind an image of Plymouth
Our one and only red and white candy-cane lighthouse.
I leave behind an image of Plymouth
The tall, standing proud cranes leaning over looking at Central Park.
I leave behind an image of Plymouth
The bright blue sparking water of the ocean
This city, this place, my home.

Megan Hand
Age 10

Dear Diary,

We've just boarded the ship and I'm more than excited
to go and start a new life. The weather is beautiful, and I
can just see the glow of the sunset over the horizon as the
harbour slowly fades away in the distance. The sparkling
water as shiny as a diamond.

Love, Matilda.

Matei Iacoban
Age 10

The New World

She turned her gaze upon the misty sea and caught a small glimpse of a marshy and caster sugar snow-covered land. A draft of cold wind circled the decks and gave her goosebumps. As the *Mayflower* drifted towards the snowy land, the crew realised they had arrived during a deep winter and had not been prepared for the chilly conditions. Hard work and difficult labour awaited boys, girls and adults. The New World created a dilemma about how they could survive and cope with the climate and inhabitants.

Days passed and they worked hard at building houses and cabins for people to live in. You could hear the knocking of nails sticking into the wood to create the frames of the lodges. Glowing fires reassured the visitors that heat and warmth could keep them from danger and food would soon fill their yearning stomachs once they finished working.

Connie Cotton
Age 10

Artwork by Connie Cotton
Age 10

The Sea

I can feel the slippery decking
I can see the waves crashing
I can see the rough sea
I can smell rotten food
I can taste sea water, this is what
I think

Rae Mossford
Age 5

The Ocean is a Canvas

The ocean is a canvas,
With the sky its paintbrush,
The sunset burns into crimson tides,
Faded stars burst through murky depths,
Jagged rocks are worn from brutal waves,
Sea foam reflects the darkening sky
Fine grains of sand no longer shine.

Dawson Brodin
Age 13

Artwork by
Nathan Annetts
Age 9

The Deep Blue Sea

Staring into the deep, blue sea,
The mysterious horizon beckons me,
Surrounded by contemplation,
Beyond the horizon is our destination.

Ruthless storms start to stir,
Worse than there ever were,
Mariners are starving, they long for food,
We've barely left home, this isn't good.

Lives are lost in a treacherous storm,
Ferocious, hammering, battering waves form,
Crumbling stern turns side to side,
Almost splitting the hull open wide,

Storms start to move across,
Half of the sailors were at a loss,
We're almost there – hope starts to rise,
The journey ahead is their prize.

Natalya Affek
Age 10

The Poet in Me

My inner poet is like a beast.
Lurking in my stomach.
It's a gentle beast, not a vicious one.
It's a good-looking beast,
Not a hideous one.
It hides behind my organs,
Like a tiger about to pounce
When the beast catches its meal,
An idea sparks in my mind.
Ideas flow again,
Like rain dripping from a gutter.
Drip. Drip. Drip.
When the beast has finished its meal,
It's full,
Nothing is going through its brain,
Like my mind,
Out of fuel.
Unable to think anymore.
But thankfully,
My poem,
Is finished.

Bryan Lehmann
Age 12

Sunrise

Barefoot
The twigs press gently against my feet
Great are the pines in their majestic solitude
The silence of the summer forest lingers
I bound to the gap in the trees
I gaze up and wonder
The sunrise breaks into my view
The earth takes a breath of morning air
Everything is peaceful
The old ashes of the fire lay motionless
The lake waits
Ready
I wait and watch the sunrise and think to myself,
This is where I am meant to be.

Scarlett O'Farrell
Age 12

Dear Diary,

Well, today has been tough because of a torrential downpour of rain and a storm. Poor Ma and Lizzie, my sister, were so downhearted. I felt like I'd never see the light of day again! The waves were high, steep and crashing. I felt like I was locked in an unhygienic chamber forever, until Ma held me close and told me it would be over soon. She sang me an old Bible song, my favourite.

I loved her and Lizzie more than anyone else, I could not lose them. I am crying at the thought. The storm was hurtling things about on our deck. Little James got hit by a barrel, poor thing. His cut was oozing with blood, but Lizzie wrapped up the cut with her lace hanky, it was all she had. She's the only nurse on board. James's screams were loud and unbearable. You couldn't hear yourself think. I just thought how lucky I'd be if I made it to the New World.

Goodbye, thank God I'm alive.

Bethany Prowse
Age 9

The Figurehead

The beautiful mermaid, swishing through the sea,
Is used as a figurehead, up front for all to see.
She is the first to spy,
The evil enemy ships as they pass by.
She was placed upon the *Mayflower*,
It makes them intimidating and gives them power.

She sniffs the salty ocean,
As the crew members cause a commotion,
There were two boats with many decks,
Fortunately, they didn't both end up as shipwrecks
As she listens to the songs of the sea,
She just wishes that someone would set her free.

Scarlett Aubury
Age 11

Artwork by Scarlett Aubury
Age 11

Beyond the Horizon

Beyond the horizon,
I leave behind an image of Plymouth.
The silhouette of Smeaton's Tower
Is celebrating the city's power.
This red and white Christmas jumper
Is a beacon guiding the lost to safety.

The wilderness of great Drake's Island
Is protecting South Devon's homeland.
The pencil grey Mayflower Steps
Lead people down to the aqua-marine water.

Along the top, you can see
The glassiness of the raging sea.
When you walk along the Barbican,
You can see the coast of England!

Elliot Mair
Age 10

Journey to the New World

Nervously, we took our first steps onto the boat.
Already I had a bad feeling,
The ship was shaking.
So, we set off to the New World.

As the journey began, it got scarier,
As a storm hit midway through.
All the shelters got cramped, but I was in a small shelter.
It kept me safe for the hours it had taken to get here,
The whistling sound of the wind made the boat wobble.

At last we arrived in the New World. So, we stopped to have food.
We had dried meat and fish, grains, flour, fruit, cheese, hard biscuits and other
foods with us.

We had to eat the food we brought until we could plant and harvest a garden
But we caught and ate fish and wild game once we landed in the New World.

Liam Dann
Age 11

Plymouth Harbour

As she stepped into Plymouth Harbour the first thing she noticed was the strong, pungent smell of fish rushing up her nostrils. Elizabeth took one final stroll along the harbourside's cobbled road before setting off for the New World. Many people were jostling around trying to buy things from the fishmonger's stand.

As Elizabeth sauntered around the corner, she saw the three mighty masts of her transport. It was the *Mayflower*. The crew were wandering around on the deck, making the final preparations before the vast vessel cast off. The hull was wooden and an immensely deep chestnut colour. Walking up the gangway, a crowd began to gather. Elizabeth waved one more farewell before she disappeared below deck.

In the heat and humidity of the lower decks, Elizabeth barely noticed that the *Mayflower* had begun to move, however she could feel it. As quick as a flash, Elizabeth dumped her bags on the floor and hurried up the stairs. Looking over the port side, Elizabeth saw that the crowd had almost tripled in size. Waving frantically, she shouted to her family, "Goodbye!"

After a few minutes, Plymouth had disappeared from view. Now the only thing between her and The New World was the open ocean.

Tom Jane
Age 10

An Agonising Typhoon at Sea

Gazing into the trembling sea,
I can feel the distance beckoning me,
Demolishing waves violently crash,
While the ruthless rain and thunder thrash.

Reckless winds beat loud like a drum,
Mystery to those brave Pilgrims, the time has come,
What on earth's going to happen next?
The storm will take over before there's time to rest.

White horses clash against the well-known shore,
For these sacred people, their home is no more,
The waves shatter the boat like Thor's hammer,
While some fearful mariners begin to stammer.

Destroying me, the helpless and lonely boat,
Wondering if I'll sink or float
As the Speedwell left me, I'm on my own,
While terrified sailors wail and moan.

Disease and sickness fill the crew,
This story now starts to feel so very true,
Pull through guys - we're losing everyone,
Fear is high! Only hope belongs to some.

Sienna Deaton
Age 10

Catherine Street is believed to have been named after Catherine of Aragon, Henry VIII's first wife, upon her arrival to Plymouth in 1501.

Dear Diary,

The day has come. It's finally time to board the *Mayflower* and head out for a new life in the New World. The ship has been cleaned and is ready for boarding. We've all got our bags packed and full of the essentials.

To be honest, I'm very nervous. I'm worried that we could encounter some horrific storms. But I overheard the Captain saying that the weather is fine. I'm very excited to create a new life.

All my love, Mary

Dear Diary,

The sea is beautiful. Dolphins and fish swim alongside us. The waves are calm, and the wind is light. This trip feels like paradise. The crew are happy, and the ship is in great condition.

All my love, Mary.

Tobias McClean
Age 9

Dear Diary,

Today is the day. Finally, we get to start a new life in the New World. Our bags are packed ready for later. I don't really know how to feel about this, I'm really excited to start a new life but I feel a tiny bit nervous. My brother is terrified, he has never been on a boat before. What if he gets seasick? My mum and dad aren't nervous at all, they think moving will make our lives better. In a couple of hours, we are going to be boarding the *Mayflower*. I will miss Holland but it's all for the best. We have been praying that God will be on our side all the way through this journey. We are about to start a new chapter of our lives.

Love, Elizabeth.

Tiana Allen
Age 10

Beyond the Horizon

I am waiting on the steps
I can smell the sand
I can smell the seaweed
I feel a bit sad because I have to leave my friends
I can see all the people on the *Mayflower*.

William Barter
Age 5

Artwork by Emillie Butler
Age 9

Doomed Souls

Lightning, thunder,
Starving hunger,
The elusive storm won't end.

All hope is drained,
As the billowing waves,
Clash and claim lives as their's.

Tilting, rolling,
Protesting, moaning,
Yet it keeps on going!

The *Mayflower*'s courage glows,
The sea keeps devouring though,
Crew pray, muted by noise.

Finally, a blessing arrives,
As it beaches, happiness thrives,
Unknowing more hell will rain down.

Tilting, rolling,
Protesting, moaning,
Yet it keeps on going!

Ruby Abrams
Age 11

A Night at Buckland

The hairs on my body stood on end but weirdly, I was nervously excited and ready to see what adventures were ahead. My first priority was to turn the lights back on so I could uncover the hidden secrets of Buckland Abbey and unfold the mysteries of Sir Francis Drake.

After half an hour of searching, I finally found a light switch, which was a relief because every time I heard a sound, I jumped! A strange, rumbling noise rang in my ears, I realised I was hungry; I had to find something to eat, so on my way I went. The longer I searched, the hungrier I got; floor after floor, I found nothing. I reached the floor where Big Frank was. By now, I was hungrier than ever before. I was still searching when I heard a deafening bang! Was someone here?

I cautiously peered around the corner and discovered that Big Frank was nowhere to be seen! Bang! I spun around and he was right there with a grin on his face. I didn't know what to do; I stood there frozen.
He whispered, "What are you doing here?"
I stumbled on my words "I... I was locked in. How are you alive?"
"I come alive every night, have you not heard of the legend?"

After my nerves calmed down and I relaxed, we had a good conversation; he even showed me where some food was hidden. We sat down in the garden, eating our food, talking about our families. I presumed he was lonely on his own, but he told me that he sees so many people in the daytime that he can't wait for peace and quiet in the night. All this talk about family made me think about my mum, so I started crying.

Big Frank wanted to help me, so we came up with a plan. I went first to make sure nobody was around because we couldn't let Frank be seen. In the distance, I saw my mum's car, I knew we had to act fast! I called him over and we set our plan in action; he lifted me onto his shoulders. I grabbed the top of the gate and heaved myself over it. As I ran towards my mum, I looked over my shoulder. Me and Frank winked at each other knowing that I'd see him again, but we would take this secret to the grave.

Hollie R
Age 10

Beyond the Horizon

There was no coming back,
Ship launching, lurching forward.
Fear gripped my heart,
This was a true journey.

Boat plunging into darkness,
I began to sweat heavily.
I felt dazed,
It was hard to breathe.

Mythical beasts were roaming the land,
Elegant birds chirping.
I felt the hard scales of serpents
And the fiery breath of phoenixes.

Diego Lerro
Age 11

The National
Armada Memorial was
unveiled in October
1890 by Admiral HRH
The Duke of Edinburgh
on behalf of Her Majesty
Queen Victoria.

Dear Diary,

It is Father's last day home. He will be leaving in less than an hour. The ship has just pulled into the bay. Father is ordering his crew around and flags are being raised. I cling onto Father like I'll never let go, but I know I'll have to. Life will be tough without him, Mother is already sick with worry. Tears are streaming down her face. Everybody is crying, but not me. No, my face is covered with fear and anger for Father. It is nearly time for Father to leave. I don't want to let Father go, I can't let Father go. My mother has to prise me off him, but it takes effort. Worrying so much has made her weak. Father is telling every family on the bay they will be fine. But everyone knows he doesn't know that, he can't be sure. The gigantic, strong boat pulls out of the bay. They will be back. Won't they?

Bethany Jones
Age 10

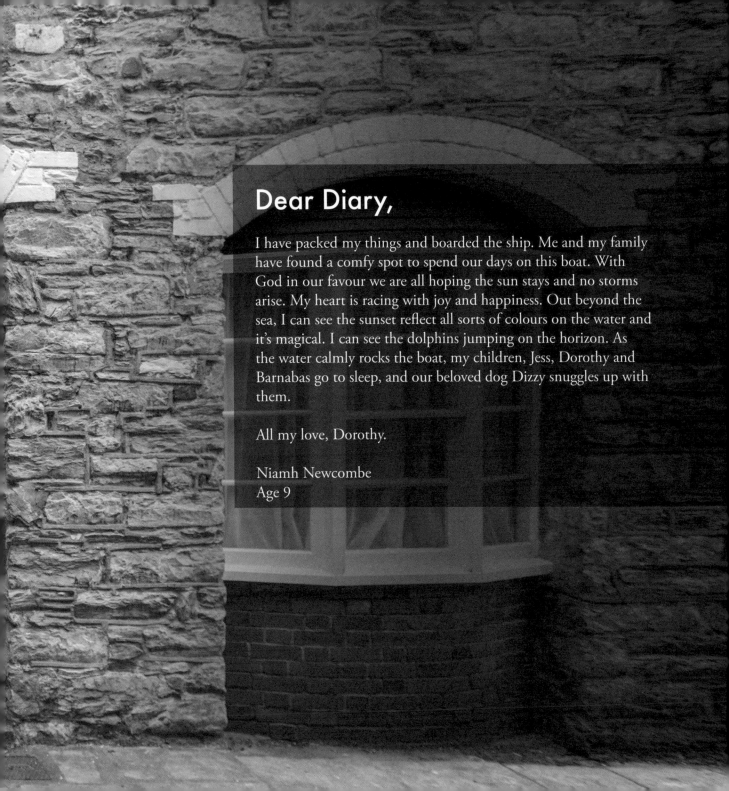

Dear Diary,

I have packed my things and boarded the ship. Me and my family have found a comfy spot to spend our days on this boat. With God in our favour we are all hoping the sun stays and no storms arise. My heart is racing with joy and happiness. Out beyond the sea, I can see the sunset reflect all sorts of colours on the water and it's magical. I can see the dolphins jumping on the horizon. As the water calmly rocks the boat, my children, Jess, Dorothy and Barnabas go to sleep, and our beloved dog Dizzy snuggles up with them.

All my love, Dorothy.

Niamh Newcombe
Age 9

Beyond the Horizon

It was a hot, sunny day. The emerald sea was shimmering against the glittering sun. As I went on the ship, I heard all the men saying that I didn't deserve to be on the ship because I am a woman. I knew I did though. Then we were off to the serene seas. I heard birds calling, I smelled salt, I tasted fish and saw the emerald water.

Connie Griffiths
Age 8

Daring Drake

Drake, Drake, Daring Drake,
One of the finest sailors one could ever make.

Spain was ruled by Prince Philip the second,
Whom Queen Elizabeth he beckoned,
She turned him down, with no heart felt,
Yet he pleaded with a heart that started to melt.

The Spanish launched their ships out in the ocean,
This they thought was their secret potion,
Prince Philip said Drake was invading the Spanish,
So he set sail to England to make him vanish.

Suddenly the Spanish appeared on the horizon, beyond the sea,
But Drake didn't panic and finished his game of bowls with glee.
With worried voices, his friends said it's time to go,
The English will not be defeated no, no, no...

Victoria Lee and Jade Bullen
Age 11 and 10

Aboard the Mayflower

Cautiously, I climbed aboard this grand ship,
Shaking hands with its Captain.
Master Christopher Jones who's as tall as a giraffe.
Who bought this beauty in 1607,
The *Mayflower*.

He commissioned the beauty,
To take us, the Pilgrims, to North Virginia,
To steadily travel with The Speedwell,
An amazing trans-Atlantic voyage,
Aboard the *Mayflower*.

Sadly, the crossing was dangerous,
The stormy seas, the super-sized waves,
Changing our course to Cape Cod,
A total of 66 days,
Aboard the *Mayflower*.

Indi Bertram-Illingworth
Age 10

Stella Maris is an ancient name for the Virgin Mary. The Stella Maris statue at the Barbican, UK is seen as a guide and protector of seafarers.

Beautiful Plymouth: The Ocean City

I look out at the Hoe and what do I see?
The sparkling sea calling out to me.
The graceful green grass dancing around,
Fancy hotels and houses in the background.
The majestic lighthouse wearing its red and white uniform,
The beautiful flowers singing to everyone.
The statues of important people reaching out to the sky,
The big waves as the bright boats go by.
The Citadel walls guarding us like grey guards,
Rows of trees standing still like soldiers.
The shining sun smiling down,
Skilful skaters, cyclists and footballers play around.
Delighted people walking excited dogs,
Others along the seafront taking a jog.
The sweet smell of the delicious ice cream vans,
Mummies pushing little babies in their prams.
The salty smell of fish and chips all around,
The loud noise of seagulls swooping down.
The waving flags dotted in empty spaces,
Smiling people chatting with suntanned faces.
Children stare as the enormous ferry glides across the
Beautiful Plymouth ocean city skyline.

Sofia Martin
Age 8

Artwork by Lois Kimber
Age 9

Beyond the Horizon

For the first half of the voyage the weather was calm,
But when storms broke out the Pilgrims came to harm.
Sailing, sailing, sailing.
One man died when he fell overboard,
Everyone else stayed cramped and bored.

All of a sudden, the crew shouted, 'land ho!'
Life would be tough, they did not know.
Sailing, sailing, sailing.
The Natives met them and greeted them well.
The Pilgrims who stayed in the New World, never said farewell.

Emmie Lawrence
Age 9

This memorial
commemorates more
than 7,200 soldiers of
World War I and nearly
16,000 of World
War II.

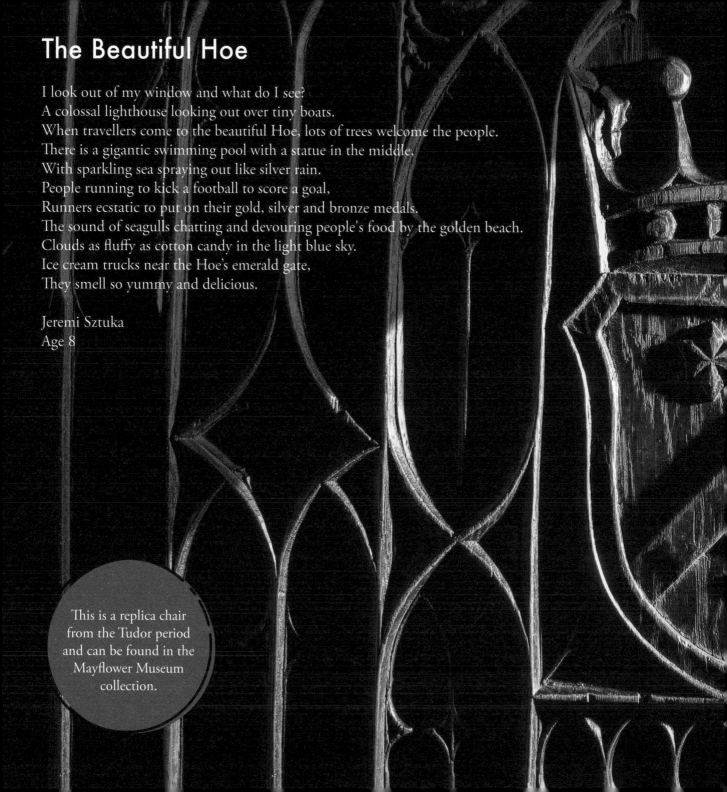

The Beautiful Hoe

I look out of my window and what do I see?
A colossal lighthouse looking out over tiny boats.
When travellers come to the beautiful Hoe, lots of trees welcome the people.
There is a gigantic swimming pool with a statue in the middle,
With sparkling sea spraying out like silver rain.
People running to kick a football to score a goal,
Runners ecstatic to put on their gold, silver and bronze medals.
The sound of seagulls chatting and devouring people's food by the golden beach.
Clouds as fluffy as cotton candy in the light blue sky.
Ice cream trucks near the Hoe's emerald gate,
They smell so yummy and delicious.

Jeremi Sztuka
Age 8

This is a replica chair from the Tudor period and can be found in the Mayflower Museum collection.

Treacherous Travels across the Atlantic

Dear Diary,
We have eventually spotted land and sailed towards it. But it wasn't the New World, it was Cape Cod! I was annoyed I came all this way and we were in the wrong place with no food. It wasn't that bad because the crew brought back juniper wood to make the ship smell better. We weren't allowed to get off the ship because of the harsh winter ahead.

Raydn Finn
Age 9

Beyond the Horizon

The ocean screams like an angry monkey.
The waves crash in the grey strong rock,
The dark, gloomy sea whispers,
The dolphins leap out of the sea.
The wooden ship crashes and bobs
Beyond the horizon.

Jack Dean
Age 7

The Stormy Voyage

Dear Diary,

It was a stormy day across the Atlantic Ocean when everyone was asleep. Some full-hard sailors were pulling the rigging but one of the sailors fell in to the raging, rushing ocean but luckily, he managed to cling on to a rock like a limpet. But when he got back on board, he got hypothermia. As we were travelling through the waves, barrels and boxes were being knocked over. Feeling excited, we got nearer to the New World, the weather became worse and worse. We met the Natives when we got to the New World. They taught us how to grow maize, corn and how to fish properly.

Nathan Annetts
Age 9

The Mayflower

I woke up exhausted from the lack of sleep I had experienced the night before. Dawn's first ray of sunlight had turned into a brilliant pink horizon. I wiped some sweat off my forehead. Realising how hot it was, I rushed past the sleeping crew members to the fresh air outside where there was a storm. The next few hours were dim, grey and uncomfortable. Lightning struck the sea just in front of the *Mayflower*. The sea started to calm down. The clouds parted to reveal a brilliant blue sky and a yellow sun. We realised it was evening. The sun started setting.

Finbar Steven
Age 7

The Most Devastating Storm

The storms have finally kicked in, the waves hurled at the ship as it smashed side to side. It was the worst storm yet; everyone's belongings went flying overboard. One man was even swept off the ship but luckily, he managed to grab a rigging rope and haul himself back on board. It was horrendous. Many hours later it had passed but everyone was afraid to go on the upper deck. One man went up and then, I heard the Captain yell "Go back beneath the decks!" So he rushed back down to the orlop deck. Luckily, we never had another storm.

Rhys Walsh
Age 9

Dear Diary,

Our bags are packed, the day is here and excited is what we are; our new life is nearly here. The ship should be arriving any moment now. I'm mostly excited but there's just this tiny bit of anxiety eating away at me. Mum and Dad think this is a unique opportunity, after all, they always say a better future lies beyond the water. We are now boarding the boat. Mum and Dad found another couple about their age and sent me lower deck. The crew warned us about the bad weather causing high waves and rough seas. Our room is cold, damp and really small, all I can hope is that God will be with us every step of the way.

From, Isabella.

Dear Diary,

The crew warned us this would happen; high seas cause rough swaying. I refuse to go upper deck. As I am writing this my heart is in my stomach. Land is in sight, but we can only just make out an outline. One of the crew members was swept off the deck, we only just pulled him up. Right now, I am on a stool in the corner of my room. The boat is just about to dock, my future is now brighter.

From, Isabella.

Isabel Sargeant
Age 11

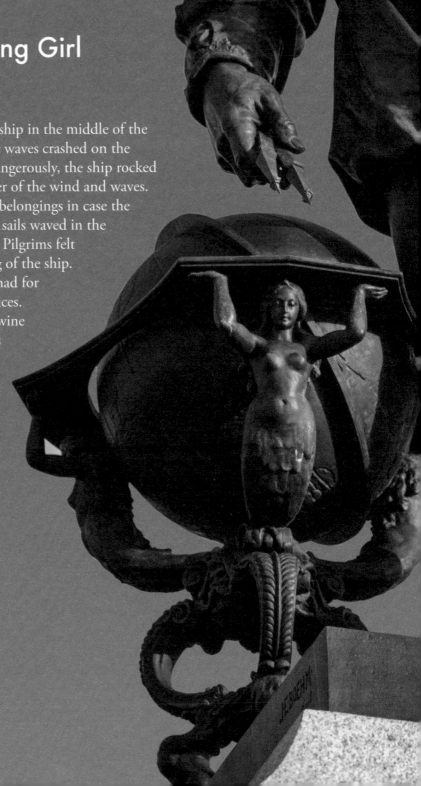

From the Eye of a Young Girl

Dear Diary,

Imagine how it would be, living on a huge ship in the middle of the
ocean for 66 days. The overactive, energetic waves crashed on the
sides of the brown, wooden *Mayflower*. Dangerously, the ship rocked
from side to side with the horrendous power of the wind and waves.
Nervously, the Pilgrims tied down all their belongings in case the
rolling waves crashed even more. The thick sails waved in the
cold wind while the tall masts wobbled. Us Pilgrims felt
very ill because of the never-ending rocking of the ship.
We barely had any food and drink. All we had for
food was rice, grains, mustard seeds and spices.
We also ate salted fish and drank beer and wine
as water went off after a week. When is this
journey ever going to end?

Louis Kimber
Age 9

On the Mayflower

When I was on the *Mayflower*,
I looked above at the sky.
I saw sparkling stars over my head,
As if they were pulling me up, up, high.

When I was on the *Mayflower*,
I looked down at the misty blue sea,
I heard the dancing, prancing waves whisper,
As if they were calling me.

When I was on the *Mayflower*,
I looked off to the side.
I saw dolphins spring out of the water,
And then the end of the tide.

When I was on the *Mayflower*,
I looked up ahead.
I saw golden sand sweeping,
And then the voices in my head.

"We did it! We did it! We're finally here!"
But then the voices left my ear.
I sunk my feet into the soft sand,
And walked across the lovely land.

Holly Melmoth
Age 8

The Tide

I am
The ocean
Ideas
Flow like the tide
Rushing
Flooding
  Onto
Shore
In a flash the paper
Engulfed in poetry
Within moments
The saturated paper is dry
All my ideas are gone
          With
        The
        Tide

Olivia Mackinnion
Age 13

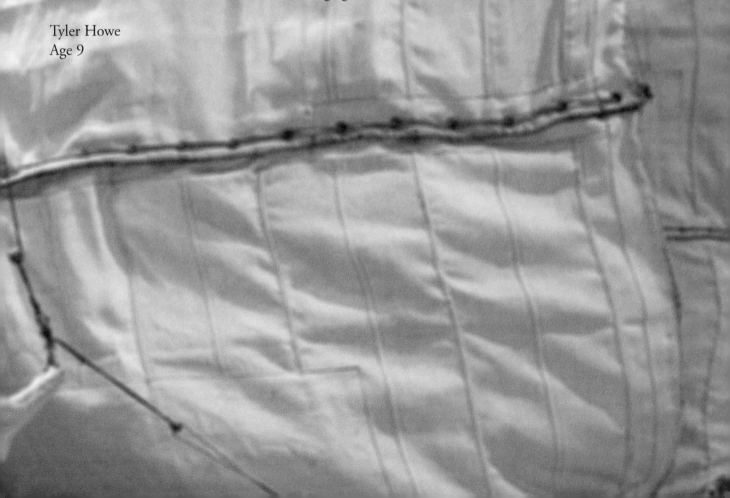

The Great Journey

Dear Diary,

We're halfway through the great voyage on the *Mayflower* and the weather is terrible. At first the weather was fine, but it got worse and worse. A couple of weeks ago, a sailor fell overboard. Luckily, he grabbed on to a rope and pulled himself up and yesterday, a baby was born. When I saw the baby, I was filled with joy. The spaniel was very energetic, but the mastiff was boring to play with. Late at night, I felt seasick – we ate grains, pottage and spices such as ginger and cinnamon. We drank beer, wine and water but water went impure within a week. At night, it was eerie because of the horrendous waves crashing against the boat.

Tyler Howe
Age 9

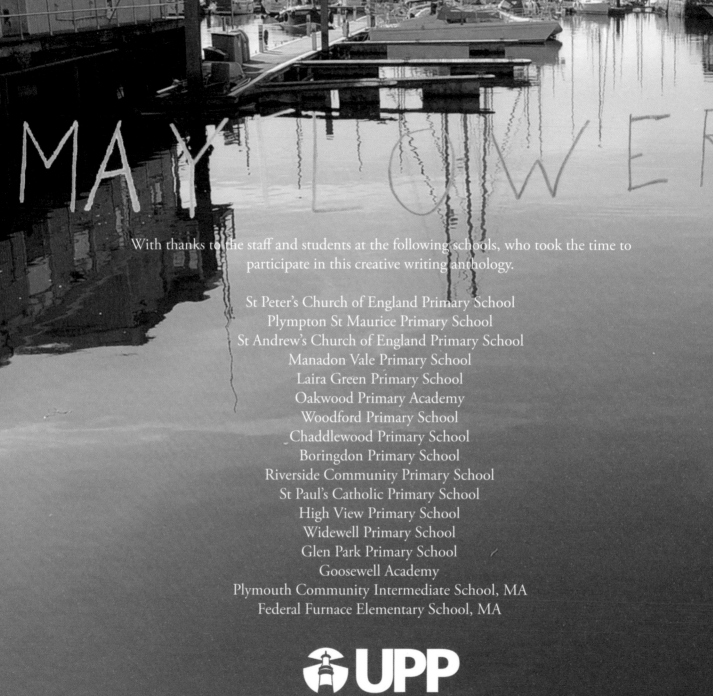

With thanks to the staff and students at the following schools, who took the time to participate in this creative writing anthology.

St Peter's Church of England Primary School
Plympton St Maurice Primary School
St Andrew's Church of England Primary School
Manadon Vale Primary School
Laira Green Primary School
Oakwood Primary Academy
Woodford Primary School
Chaddlewood Primary School
Boringdon Primary School
Riverside Community Primary School
St Paul's Catholic Primary School
High View Primary School
Widewell Primary School
Glen Park Primary School
Goosewell Academy
Plymouth Community Intermediate School, MA
Federal Furnace Elementary School, MA

University of Plymouth Press